A Wish-For Dinosaur

by Jane Belk Moncure
illustrated by Vera K. Gohman

Published by

Mankato, Minnesota

The Library —
A Magic Castle

Come to the magic castle
When you are growing tall.
Rows upon rows of Word Windows
Line every single wall.
They reach up high,
As high as the sky,
And you want to open them all.
For every time you open one,
A new adventure has begun.

Darrin opened
a Word Window.
Guess what he saw?

A dinosaur!

"Hi," said the dinosaur. "I am a
wish-for dinosaur. What is your wish?"

"I wish you would stay with me all day and be my pet," said Darrin.

"I will," said the dinosaur. So Darrin put a collar on his pet and . . .

took him home.

8

The dinosaur sat up. But he was so tall, his head bumped the roof.

Bump
Bump

The house shook.

10

Darrin's dad was painting the wall in the hall.

Bump Bump went the paint on the ladder. Guess what?

The ladder fell **Crash!**

And the paint did too **plop!**

"What a mess!" said Darrin's dad.

"Now for trick number two," said Darrin to his dinosaur.

"Lie down . . .

and roll over." But when the dinosaur rolled over,

Bump Bump

he bumped the house again.

Darrin's mom was in the kitchen.

Bump
Bump
went the dishes and the pots
and pans. Guess what?

The dishes, pots, and pans fell

on the floor. "What a mess!"
said Darrin's mom.

"One more trick," said Darrin to his dinosaur. "Fetch the ball."

Away ran the dinosaur. Guess where?

Right into the garden.

Crash Smash

What a mess!

Darrin's mom and dad heard all the noise. They ran out to the garden.

"Oh no!" they cried. "Who made all this mess?"

"This is my pet dinosaur," said Darrin.
"I am teaching him tricks."

"Not at our house!" said Mom.
"That dinosaur must go!" said Dad. So . . .

Darrin took his dinosaur to the park.

He saw this sign:

PET FAIR TODAY
Prize for best pet!

"Come along," said Darrin. "I bet we will win the prize."

Darrin saw lots of pets at the pet fair. He saw . . .

dogs,

cats,

some goldfish,

and a pretty pet parrot.

But no one had a pet as big
or as tall . . .

or as smart as Darrin's pet.

Guess who won the pet race?

Darrin's dinosaur did.

Guess who led the pet parade?

Darrin's dinosaur did.

And guess who won the blue ribbon
for the best pet yet?

Darrin's dinosaur did.

Did the kids get to play with the best pet? You bet.

They played in the park until it was dark.

Then it was time to say good-by.

"Please stay," said Darrin.

"No," said the dinosaur. "I am only a wish-for dinosaur.

You wished for me to stay all day.
And I did. Good-by."